Why can't I find Love?

Contents

Chapter 1: Personality Growth

I'm curious if it's insecurity that drowns me down to these past thoughts, why can't I find myself moving forward from these thoughts. "Why can't I find love? ". I want to learn more about myself maybe if I start loving myself first perhaps I'll get the answers. Self-awareness that's what I started with, I found myself investing most of my time and finance on some things that I don't care about. "Why ?" I asked myself that question.

I have to be honest to myself if I want answers. I feel like I was doing all this spending because I wanted to impress my peers, I wanted to put pressure on them. So they can see me as a person who is living a fancy life, a life that I can't afford. Honestly, even if I try to budget for it, I can't maintain this fancy lifestyle. I had to separate myself from these people and find people who I can grow with. I had to be friends with people who can benefit me in the future.

I realize is easy said than done. It's not easy to find people who are well disciplined and who stay true to their commitments(laughs). I guess I had to find inspiration somewhere else. YouTube! , YouTube was the solution. I watched biographies and interviews of the most influential people in the world. I had that burning desire that I felt like I can accomplish anything in the world.

Then through research of videos, I found my hobby. I wanted to write a book about all information I gathered. I'll make specific research on a subject and write a book about it.

The love of writing a book didn't take a day or 2 but a month or two of research, commitment, discipline, and hard work. I wrote 4 Novels and I wasn't satisfied at all. I wanted to write about something that I relate to, I want to write about my problem and the solution to my problem.

Emotions !, I have a problem with emotions. Sometimes I can't control my emotions. Anger and violence are my most response. I feel embarrassed sometimes because I would cause a scene instead of keeping my cool and ignoring the negative energy. I read books about emotional intelligence, and to be honest, I felt bored(laughs)because it's hard for me to apply everything there. I just feel hopeless. I took a break for a few days, so I could just cool down my mind. One thing I learned from the books I read is when coming to reacting to people's emotions. You must feel different, meaning you have to see people differently in their ways. To be able to do that you have to experience the life they are living by absorbing and analyzing why would a person react in such a manner. Sometimes the reason is because of the way we were raised or our environment.

In the afternoon, it was a sunshiny day. I was sitting outside the house under a tree just for fresh air. 10 minutes later my Uncle George and his boss dropped him off by the gate but before he got a chance to get out of the car. Uncle George's boss seemed so angry at uncle George. He was shouting, even though I couldn't hear anything they were saying in the car but the body language it was obvious that his boss wasn't happy.

Uncle George finally was dismissed by his boss. When his boss Thomas drove off, uncle George was laughing and smiling as if nothing happened. He opened the gate and he saw me. "Afternoon My nephew, " he said, " Afternoon Uncle George, what was going on with Sir Thomas ?"

" He's crazy, that's what's going on " he laughed. " I just got surprised how he controls his emotions every time. I just felt miserable that someone can do that and I can't. " Okay uncle, there is food in the oven ". He went inside the house as if nothing happened. How does this man deal with someone disrespectful? I know my uncle is a man of his own beliefs, he doesn't tolerate nonsense and he has anger. So to see him tolerant that, made me wonder how does he do that.

Maybe the answers are in front of me and I can't even see them. I think if I interact with different kinds of people I'll be able to control my emotions. Then I tried that. On the first day, I met this young girl I think she was 2 years younger than me, then I started a conversation with her. The conversation was interesting and honest. I was satisfied and happy that I met her. I even took her numbers. The second day I went somewhere different I went to a crowded place. I was leaning against the wall of the market. Then I saw this man passing by and I didn't realize he was drunk. Then I tried to make a conversation with the man. He wasn't friendly at all, the moment I greeted him he just pushed me " Get out of the way boy " he said. I was angry, then finally calmed myself down. I realize that I can't do this. I can't hold myself from all of these feelings.

What can I do? What can I do to master my emotions? I went to my uncle and finally got an opportunity to ask him? What are the secrets? Uncle George was laying down in his room, thinking ." Uncle George, I want to ask you something. I'm really curious about controlling my emotions, I want to master my emotions. I don't know why I have these forces that compile me to react to people's emotions. I've seen you control 90% of your actions. It's like you are not possessed by human emotions, how do you do that? " I asked.

Uncle George laughed and said " it's not easy my nephew you know, it takes a lot of time and practice. I had the same problem as you when I was young. I didn't have someone who can help me control my feelings and I didn't also have materials that can guide me. I finally had therapy with myself and tried to figure out something because I was an emotional person. I would get in a fight with people at school every single day. Sometimes I would get my butt whooped and sometimes I'm the one who is doing the whooping (laughs). The most important thing was I decided to stop all this nonsense before I'll get myself hurt or I'll hurt someone.

I did some research before I begin my therapy session. I needed to know how can I handle my sessions. After a week or so I had created the tools I needed for my therapy. It consists of how many hours and times I should have a therapy session with myself. I had to meditate after every session I had with myself.

I had a diary where I could write everything that was happening to me during the day. I was willing to commit so I can have control. What I have learned from the beginning of my journey was, that thinking that you are going to do something and doing something is different. Again everyone has a high chance of failure so the sooner you start the sooner you realize your mistake and fix it.

A month passed, and I realized that therapy sessions that I was having with myself, everyone is having one without realizing it. Those small talks we have with ourselves are the ones that build us daily. Sometimes it's effective when someone has made us angry or sad. We would overthink the whole scenario all over again and again. Wishing you could have done or changed something, at that moment you either choose to let it go, hold grudges, or revenge on someone. I'm telling you the process of getting a response is a therapy session, this process is very important because it determines your future.

Let's take this for an example, or let's take me for example I know this other day you saw me with my boss when he was making noise and showing no respect towards me. One could wonder how I manage to work with him. I worked for his company for over 10 years, and even today there is no respect. He treats me like an animal with no rights. When I started working for him, every day after work I would have a therapy session with myself. Honesty I wanted to quit my job, I would tell myself that I would go to him and give him my resignation letter. I keep on telling myself that, during every session I had.

One day at work my boss humiliated me in front of my colleague, he talked to me like I had no clue about life like I'm a 5 years old boy. I was provoked by an old White Man, I wanted to beat him up. I held myself, I didn't show any sign of being affected by his words. During that day at lunchtime, I was outside eating my lunch meal, I was becoming weak and weaker. I wanted to quit for real, I was forced to work so I can put food on the table. I was in emotional pain, and I wanted to confront him next time so we can talk about it. While I was sitting outside eating, a few of my colleagues came and joined me. They were impressed by how I showed no sign of fear and pain because they also know that's how he treats everyone.

Some felt inspired and some laughed. I realize that if I keep on telling myself every session I have that I wanted to quit I'll eventually do it. I had to change the subject of my content in my session. *emotions can't control me*. I will do a daily practice and have sessions of those small talks until I'm good with it.

After 3 months or so, I didn't need a routine I was used to it. I would talk to the inner me everywhere I go. I wouldn't be affected by emotions. I could control 90% of my actions that have to do with emotions. That 10% was human nature, I had to find a way to deal with it. Nephew don't worry yourself too much, just apply what I did and you'll add a few things to them. Do what works for you, okay young nephew. "

I left my uncle George's room. I thought my uncle was no man, now I see he had a way he had to see it. It's just that I wasn't around to see it. I can do my method better. He was living in an era where white people were superior, now all races are equal. Besides that, we can be disrespected most by a person who is in a higher position than us at work like how my uncle was disrespected. On a personal level (laughs) I have never seen my uncle be humbled by someone or something before. I guess life can humble all of us in different ways.

I am on my own on this journey, if I can't do it now what guarantees that I'll be able to control my feelings in the future. I began with my theory. I wanted to start by meditating for 30 days so I can be able to get used to my system. Did a working out routine for my body, reported my daily productivity results, and ate healthy all the time. I did this for another 30 days. During my meditations the was a list that I have to tick every time. The first thing I have to identify my emotions, I have hun to identify what causes me to be in this condition. Once I identified what caused it then I start to acknowledge my emotion and understand that I am a human being. 2nd On the list is I have to take responsibility, meaning sometimes I wouldn't admit that I was wrong. The reality is it's better for me to admit to myself and take responsibility for my actions. This will help to avoid making the same mistake twice.

3rd on the list was to always be open-minded and accepting that I won't know everything and always open my mind to other prospective. 4th on the list was to embrace reality, meaning sometimes I can't always win the battle of emotions. I don't have to go hard on myself and make myself feel bad because I couldn't control myself.

This is my life and my story I have to embrace it. 5th on the list was to live in the present. The past can cause us nothing but pain, in the present, you get a chance to be a person who you couldn't be in the past. After months and more of following my schedule and practice. I was physical, mental, and emotionally healthy. I realize even your lifestyle can impact your emotions too.

I think I was done with the emotional journey, I needed to continue building a great personality for myself. This is where I started to like the idea of loving and putting myself first. I Start to see that you don't need to find love in someone only, that's a secondary love, and most important is loving yourself first. You have to accept yourself and work from there. The answer to love is in yourself, you don't need money to find out what you love. You need yourself, just those little talks you have can help you in the long run.

I was doing my last year in high school. I wanted to prepare myself for the worse at college next year. I was staying with my uncle since my parents passed on in a car accident when I was young. It doesn't hurt me that much because my uncle George he always been good to me. I just feel cursed when coming to girlfriends. All girls I met are mediocrity, I don't know why I attract such girls. I believe, I mean I know there is someone out there who can appreciate me for who I am.

I take relationships very seriously, I don't why, maybe I'm not like other boys, or am I living in my imagination? Let it be if it's so. I won't be living here on earth to be a follower, I'm a leader too. I will do and get what I want because I deserve it. (Laughs) I guess I'm overreacting now but I'm being honest with myself. I have to work for it, if I don't get it, I'll try my best potential to get it.

Finally, the year was ending, I'm feeling scared because I'll be far from home and the is a high chance for all my friends to go to a different town. I have to stand by my own and be my own man. I'm more worried about getting a bursary because my uncle George doesn't earn that much. I promise him one day I'll help him with financials, I didn't just promise him that. I promise him the world, everything he ever wanted to have when he was a child.

My last month at school was painful to see a girl I loved moving forward with someone else, honesty I have to move on. It is easy said than done. I wasn't sure I was ready to move on. I had something that was missing from me. I had no idea what it was. I saw my ex-girlfriend after school walking with this guy in my English class. It felt like nothing but a curse but I kept my cool and acted as if I have never seen them.

I CAN'T BELIEVE IT, I just witness my ex with someone. I never imagine how hard it will be to move on I guess these small talks I have with myself I have to change it and try to find someone of my own, someone who I can share my life with. We all need love and I should stop thinking that all girls are the same.

My best friend Max invited me over for his birthday party, he was having the house by himself. My uncle George luckily was going out that weekend, I don't quite remember where. I was happy I could be free to go out. Max is a wild friend and he's fortunate enough to have both parents who are both earning a lot of money. His parents went oversea for their anniversary and he took the opportunity I don't blame him though. I will do the same if I was him.

I went to his house in the afternoon so we can prepare for the night. He bought booze for over 10K, he bought other needs for that party that cost 7 K. I was so excited for the night. The invitation was fire, everything was a fire. 6 pm people started to show up, around 7 pm it was so packed and lit. I was amazed how we made the whole setup fire for everyone.

On my way to the bathroom, I saw this beautiful girl, I couldn't take my eyes off her. I was drunk in love I went to the bathroom and did my business, I was hoping I can find her in the spot where I left her. I went outside the bathroom. Luckily I found her at the same spot but this time she was surrounded by her friend. I was doubting if I should go and say hi. I didn't wanna seem desperate, I gave her eye contact and went back to my crew. We drank booze, we danced and we had fun.

People were smoking and popping drugs, it was the best night of my life. I told max to tell people who are doing drugs to go out, he wasn't taking my words too seriously perhaps he knows that they are addicted. I was so drunk, that I was even sweating. The booze was about to be finished, we divide the booze into 3 groups. The starting, midnight, and end of the party booze. I was about to hand over the midnight booze, I found that girl outside the room freezer together with her crew of friends.

"Hello, ladies, " I said with a smile, "Hi" they all responded. "What y'all doing here? " I said. They laughed and one of the girls responded " we want booze, the booze is finished ". I laughed and said, " Woah ! So y'all planning to take all the booze for yourselves? No this ain't how it works . I'm gonna hand it over to everyone fairly . "

They were giggling and the girl I gave eye contact with early on responded " hey what's your name? You cute ". "Woo" her friends made comments, I laughed, blushed aside, and responded " I go by the name of Ben and you are cute yourself . You know what I think, I have the key for this freezer. What about we go inside together because I can see your friends don't appreciate me "we both blushed. One of her friends argued softly " why her ? " I ignored her and continue talking to the girl " so what's your name? ". She responded, " my name is Pamela ". I opened the freezer, left the key on the door, and responded " So Pamela get inside with me only here please " she smiled and we both got inside the freezer. One of her friends Fridah got bitter and locked us inside the freezer. I think her friends were already drunk. Boom!! a door slammed and closed. " Fridah !! Open the door, this is not funny at all, we gonna freeze to death, " Pamela said. Fridah replied" Only if I put the temperature average so you two can be able to cuddle " she laughed.

I kicked the door angrily " open the damn door, girls!!! ". I checked my phone there was no network, I was starting to lose it. Pamela came behind my back and tried to comfort me. " I'm sorry about my friends, don't get angry it won't help, just hold me so we can keep each other warm " she held me. I felt better instantly, I smiled a bit. She stared at me straight in my eyes and kissed me. I was so happy that that moment happened, she was all over my body the whole time. We were able to talk about everything, our childhood, our past, our present, and our future.

I felt lucky for that moment that I found someone with who I can bond for, the rest of my life. She was everything I ever wanted.

Fridah finally opened the door for us. "Hi guys are fine," said Fridah. "we're more than fine but what you did wasn't cool at all okay, I didn't like it, " said Pamela. I can't be quiet because I was blinded by love. I just let it slide, I thought I was going to give Fridah a taste of her own medicine. Things turned out the way I wasn't expecting.

I INVITED FRIDAH IN so she can help me with handing out alcohol for the guests, we did that and left most alcohol to us. We were all drunk, I started to realize I couldn't take it anymore. I asked Pamela to accompany me to the guest room, and she did and we went to the room and slept.

Early in the morning, " wakey wakey" I heard a voice coming from somewhere, I couldn't indicate where is the voice coming from . " wakey wakey" she said again, my eyes slowly opened. The moment I woke up, I saw Pamela staring at me and blushing. I was so excited, I couldn't resist myself and I blushed too. She kissed me on my forehead and said "Good morning ". I covered my mouth and responded "Good morning Princess" she smiled and we woke up and help out with the cleaning of the house.

Honesty the house was a mess, we had to buy paint and repaint certain spots. If it was me who hosted this party my uncle was going to kill me. We finished cleaning the house and Max had an idea that we have the last chilling party with me and Pamela's group of friends. It allowed me to build a bond with Pamela.

What happened this night was more than a bond, I was so excited. Max suggested we go to the nearest local cheap Pub since he was low on cash since I was depending on him financially. Pamela was becoming a little bit cold on me on our way to the pub and I asked her " what's wrong Honey ?". She said "nothing baby " and I saw her she try to avoid me. " I can see you a bit upset, you know you can talk to me about everything. I'm here for you. " I said. She looked at me in my eyes and said " Are you serious that you not seeing someone ? I'm sorry to be insecure but you know how boys are ? The next thing they have a baby mama and the next he's cheating ". "I understand baby, you just met me and you are not sure if you can trust me. I assure you that I'm loyal to you. I love you. I do feel different when I'm with you. I know it might be hard to believe it but I'm willing to show you through my action. Pamela to be honest with you, it's hard to accept we met at a house party and we fell in love there.

I want to accept the fact that it's possible. I know I deeply love you, the question is are you deeply in love with me as I do ?" I said. Pamela blushed as we reached the pub and got inside the pub. Max and I separated in directions and he went with the girls to find the right spot for us to chill the whole night. Max gave me his credit card before we separated inside the pub. I bought a lot of booze for the rest of the night.

When I got to the spot that max chose, Pamela was smiling and blushing while staring at me. "Ladies here is the booze, " I said. I went to sit next to Pamela unfortunately she's had to sit on my lap since the were no available chairs. She looked me in the eyes and I said " You haven't answered my question ". She kissed me for a long time and said " Does this answer your question ". I said " I guess it does babe, It does " I was drowning inside a sea of love. Why does it feels so good at the beginning and feels like it's going to end badly at the end?

Her favorite song played and she asked me if I could dance with her. I'm not a good dancer I'll just stand behind her and let her shake for me (laughs) that's the plan. She dance until the song finish playing, I held her close to me and kissed her. We had a lot of fun, I never felt so alive since I broke up with my previous ex-girlfriend.

[Pamela and I]

[Pamela and I at the dance floor]

[The time Pamela realize that I was drunk and had enough]

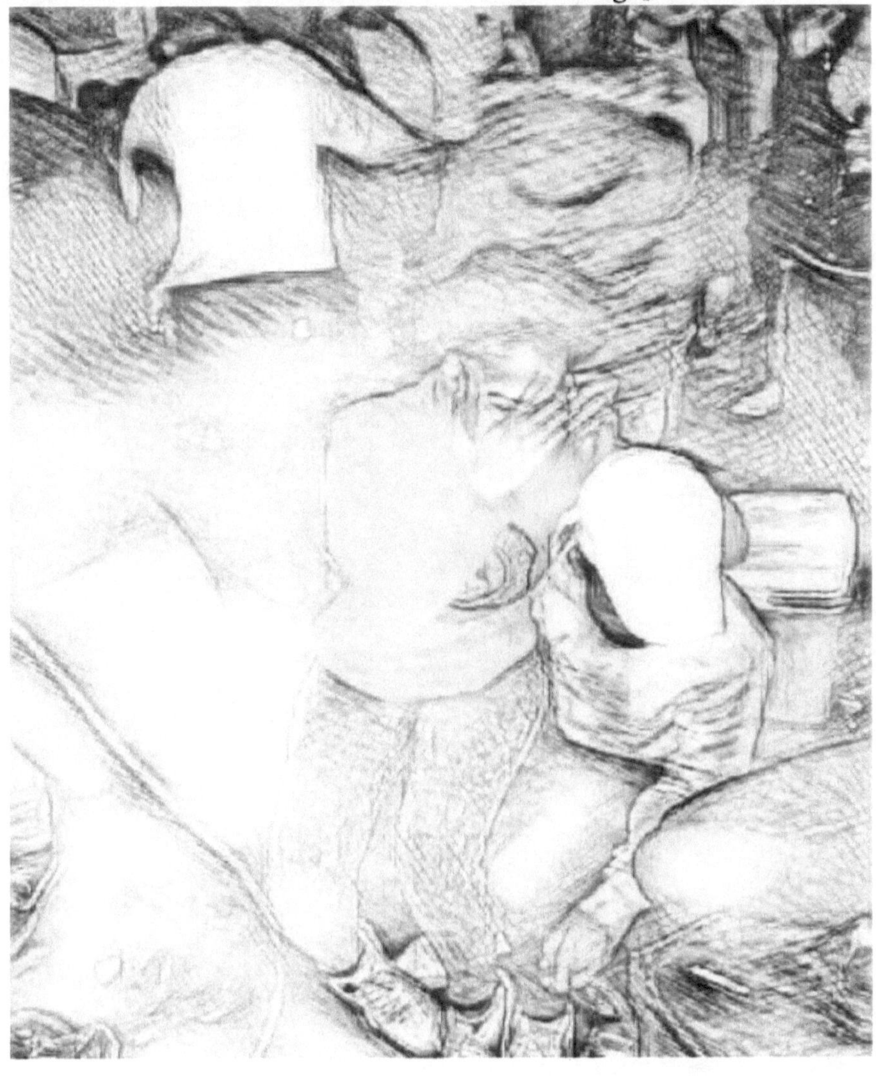

[Pamela and her friends]

WE WENT BACK TO SIT down, this is the moment where I realized that I'm too drunk. I didn't want to seem weak. I kicked a bottle of booze that I left on the side of my chair by mistake, luckily the bottle didn't break. Pamela threw that bottle and gave me another bottle of beer to avoid drinking small pieces of a bottle that might be broken inside. Pamela was sitting on my lap the whole time, she put the bottle on the floor. I took my time and I felt like drinking the last bottle.

When I was about to pick up the bottle of beer I couldn't. I tried I couldn't, it felt so heavy.

Pamela started to take notice, she begins to laugh and she covered her face with her hands indicating that she saw how weak I am. " baby what's wrong ?" She said. I looked away like I'm not paying attention. "Baby I think we should go, I think you had enough, " she said. " I agree, " I said. She called max to come closer to tell him that we want to leave and he must call a cap driver. He did so and we left, I couldn't walk or even feel my legs. They had to carry me to the bed, Pamela and I slept on the same bed while others took the guest rooms.

[*I was dreaming, I was in a car with my parents, driving back home. We passed at the garage to fill up the gas. My dad was outside smoking a cigarette, mom was with me inside the car and I was in the backseat .she said to me staring at the front mirror of the car facing my dad "I wish your father could stop smoking you know, this is bad. I talked to him. I know it's getting hard sometimes for him I understand. I just hope he finds a way to meditate his problems into peace because smoking is not just bad for his health but his finance ". My dad came back in the car and we were ready to go. On our way we were playing classic songs, my dad is a fan of the 70s he likes to keep it too jazzy that's what he always says. We stopped at the stopped sign waiting for another vehicle to cross first, my mom turn around to the back seat and said "I love you, son, so much "my dad shifted his head for a moment and said " we love you so much son "my dad moved the car slowly in the same position and continued" I know you smart very smart, I hope one day you become a better man I was . I know you'll........" a truck came and crashed us.]*

I woke with a scared heartbeat, Pamela woke up immediately and held me ." Don't worry everything is going to be alright " she grabbed me back to sleep. It was Sunday morning I woke up and woke Pamela up ." baby I got to go home my uncle must be worried about me, " I said. She Kissed me, gave me her number, and said " we'll talk on a cell phone call babe, bye " and she went back to sleep. I jogged home so my uncle can get home before me.

Luckily when I got home he wasn't there. I took a little rest until my uncle came back. In the afternoon my uncle came back the first thing he did was a cup of tea. He's a tea person. I went to the kitchen " hi uncle " I said. He responded " Hi nephew, how was your weekend? I hope you didn't hide any girl in my house. If you did tell her to go out now because I wanna sleep " I laughed and said " I promise no one is in the house and tell me about you and how was your weekend ? " he told me everything about his weekend, how he learned new things and how it felt like a holiday away to him.

Honestly, I'm happy that he enjoyed his weekend, it's nice to see an old man having fun after a long time.

I was thirsty for a soda, so I decided to go to the shop to get one for myself. I got to the shop-bought my fav soda I couldn't wait to drink it at home and decide to drink it on my way home.

When I was about to close the bottle. My right eye saw the face structure of Pamela's face. I stopped and the car was across the road, they stopped too. It was indeed Pamela with an older guy. I witness them kissing and him giving her money.

Is my eyes deceiving me ? Am I seeing what I'm seeing here ? Am I dreaming ? I don't know what should I take from that bond we had , I don't if I will ever find true love from someone . Why every girl I met are playing me ? Why ? Why ? Please oh Lord tell me why ? I stood there and had many thoughts .

Can someone just come to me and help me move my legs so I can go home .

MY WORLD WAS SHATTERED, my heart fell and broke down into tiny pieces. I felt a tear falling down my eyes and immediately went home. I didn't understand if this was luck or a curse. This is the moment where I have to apply that method of mine the small talk.

I know this hurts me a lot, I want to learn to accept the situation the way it is and focus on what I can change. She didn't deserve me I understand that they might be financial issues that I had to fix with myself. I understand a woman is always seeking safety and security. I couldn't give Pamela that, it won't be easy but I am willing to walk the steps of improving myself to be a better man one day. This is just the beginning for me I'm growing I'm 18 years old. I'm willing to show the world what I have on me for them. I'm so lucky I have to experience pain through my relationship to see that these small talks we have daily with ourselves build up slowly. It's a small investment, more like a business starting from small investments to bigger investments. When I mean lucky I mean some people experience the worse scenario like abuse, trauma, accidents, death loss, etc. On my side, I could say I accept that both my parents are gone and I found peace in myself. If one is being arrested or raped perhaps when at that moment they must understand those small talks they have every day is the one that grows them in that direction. Meaning if a raped girl can't stop talking about what happened and how bad she wants to hurt him it will take a long time for her to heal. If she decides to work her calendar out and mark which day she will be fit to do certain things, take baby steps, and always have small talks that she won't let things get her down. Learning how to accept what happened and improve herself maybe also join a self-defense class. Yes, it is not easy but at least you can do it, take a small step at a time. I wish everyone can do it like me investing in small talks, taking action, experiencing, and fixing my mistake. At the same time, I'm learning that I haven't yet mastered my emotion but see that emotion is long-term learning. The small talks are the small steps to mastering my emotions.

Finally, I graduated from high school, it was the biggest day of my life. My uncle was there to show me support. I took pictures with my friends and uncle George didn't want to be in the pictures. He said this is my time not his. This is an achievement in my life that I should remember one day how it feels when I'm not operating fine and thinking of quitting.

It should be a reminder and be one of the reasons why I should work hard despite my current/future failures.

This should be a new topic in my next book (personality growth) where I use the small talks we have in ourselves to grow a personality. I start to understand that this method of small talk you can use in every field of your life. It's not easy but you should always try to solve your issue to avoid small talk to grow your personality.

IT WAS DECEMBER ALREADY, one month left before the year-end. I was standing outside the house just watching people passing in the street. My uncle arrived home early, he didn't seem very well. He went inside the house. After half an hour I decided to go inside the house and check on him. I found my uncle sleeping in bed, " Uncle George, what's wrong? I said. My uncle responded " I'm not okay son, I don't know how should I put this. I wasn't feeling well at work and my supervisor realized that. He decided to take me to sickbay and they ran a few tests, my results came and I was HIV positive."

I was in shock honesty, I was feeling very sorry for him. I start to realize that I have to be a man and take care of my uncle. I knew he won't last in the factory. I had some small talks with myself that moment that I had to look for a part-time job next year. So my uncle can rest and stay healthy. I joined my uncle in bed, hugged him, and slept. He wasn't very comfortable with the hugging but it was fine I just laid down on the bed and took a nap with him.

24 December before Christmas I was standing beside my Uncle George's tombstone, tears couldn't resist coming out. I felt a pain that I never felt in my life. Pain that I have no choice but to deal with alone. I wish I had seen it coming. I want to avoid talking about this pain but I can't because I love him. I was looking for love all the time and asking myself why don't I find love? And love was in front of me the whole time. Uncle George loved me, he took care of me like his own son. I should have appreciated his love, I should learn how to appreciate. I should learn how to accept that he's passed away(cries) and move forward. He forever going to be in my heart. That man he's a true Uncle, I miss him so much. Yes, Indeed I found love through my Uncle George. Now I see how how important family is .

I had to move with my mother's sister. It was a pretty cool place, I enjoyed myself my first week there. The lawyer came home and he brought great news for me. On uncle George's will he wrote that I should have all his money(insurance claims, pension, savings, etc)and his house. He also requested I sell the house and start my own life with the money. I couldn't believe my eyes. I had great plans for my future. I sold the house and the money I received together with the policy was 6 million. I was very happy I didn't know things will turn up this way. My uncle was a rich man wow, we were staying in a small 3 bedroom house while he had millions. This gives me a different perspective that our parents were also young and had dreams like us but chose to sacrifice them so we can build a better one than theirs. Uncle George and I used to watch this reality show where people are interviewed about how they spend all their millions in a year and went broke. I have no idea why he loved that show but I think he wanted to show me how I shouldn't spend my money like them.

I didn't tell my aunt Becker how much I received the money in total what she knows is I received millions according to her calculations. She kept on asking me I told her it was a secret and she would laugh. I kept the money in the savings until I had a plan of what should I do with it. One day I was sitting and watching tv during the day, my Aunty Becker came home drunk I could see her through the window. She was with a young girl helping her to walk her home. " Open the door this is my house! " Aunty Becker said at the door. The girl opened the door and I went to help out " stop helping me, no one wants to help me " she said. "Why would you say such aunt," I said, " who do you think to pay for the electricity, where do you think this b food you eat comes from. You just got money and you did nothing for me, you haven't given me any cent. So stay out of my way I'm going to sleep" she said and walked away.

The girl my aunt came with was shocked and she said " it's alright hey, she is drunk and don't take it seriously " she hugged me and asked me to take a sit. I was shocked thinking maybe she might be right(guilty conscious), I understand that we all want to feel like we are moving forward. I felt like I should just create a small business that my Aunty can at least make extra income with. " Can I get you water? Oh, my name is Tracy, your aunt and I are close " she said. "Close? How? You are like the same age as I am and young obviously " I said. She smiled and laughed" you know our neighborhood is very small so everyone knows one another, you must be Benjamin and you're cute, " she said and blushed. I smiled back and said " Just call me Ben, really do you tell everyone you just first met that ? ", she smiled and giggled " no come on, you know what I mean, what about we go chill at the park ? There is a perfect park nearby where we can chill and have some fresh air, " she said. " Cool let's go, you'll show me around too since I'm new here, " I said.

We went to the park, she showed me places where I could get anything I need like clubs, booze, and weed. I guess that's what teenagers are interested in. We sat on the grass talked and bonded. She was so open about everything, she just wants someone she can trust and be with. It's too early to tell what she wants. I want to be close with her as friends and see where it leads to.

I want to shower her with gifts and love. I want to communicate my love language through her. Luckily the pandemic hit (Codvid 19)this is an opportunity for me to see if she is the right person. If she wants to spend her whole life with me. if she is not the one, it's just a journey I'll finally get my victory at last I'm patient. Honestly, I'm sad my uncle is gone, I have to appreciate the other part that I have 6 million in a bank just laying there and only myself and the lawyers know about it. Then there is Tracy here a nice beautiful-looking girl, wow life is mysterious I wish I could talk about this whole relationship with my uncle I guess now I got Tracy and my aunt Becker. I remember how I promised my uncle George the world I guess now I have to fulfill that promise to my aunt Becker.

Some people tend to lie a lot and never tell the truth. They would ask themselves "why can't they find love ?" I guess their portrait lies and that will be their results. A few min later when I was about to leave the park with Tracy I received a shocking message from Max " I can't do this anymore, it's been very hard for me to overcome the sickness that's upon me. I'm seeing and feeling unnatural things. I don't know how to explain them to you because they are more like sci-fi. I'm sorry for taking this selfish decision. I'm sorry I hope your writing journey be successful. Please be strong and patient. Don't be weak like me. I love you like my brother. I'm sorry, Love Max "

I was so shocked and scared. I tried to call max and it was too late. He committed suicide, I couldn't hold my tears. I was just floating in a river of my tears. It didn't make sense to me because Max comes from a rich fortune family, he just graduated from high school I'm sure he was going to the most expensive University overseas. What might I be missing? He said sci-fi things, I don't understand. I thought I had everything figured out but I didn't. Tracy realise that I was in pain, I was numb. She didn't want to ask me a lot of things but took me home and gave me space.

I think she saw how overwhelmed I was, that's why she wasn't talking so much.

I slept for hours, I didn't want to wake up. I felt depressed. Honestly, I was feeling like taking a vacation somewhere where I can be able to erase my feelings and forget about everything. I had the money to do so but I knew, it was my weak thoughts talking. Day by day I was trying to forget about my friend max, when I try to do so I start to have flashbacks about my Uncle George. I'm starting to lose it, I'm starting to feel like those small talks I'm having with myself are affecting me and I can't stop being negative. What can I do? What can I do to defend myself from these overwhelming emotions and thoughts? I'm losing my strength and hope. I want something that can make me sleep. I'm thinking too much of trying drugs. I'm aware that these small talks are very toxic for me and on the other hand I'm thinking too much of using the money recklessly. I don't know if I can hold myself till I fully recover.

I have to think like a king, I had to put one investment thoughts somewhere where it can determine a better chance of a better future for me. When a king is about to lose a war/battle he retreats his troops back to the palace so he can come up with a better plan, a smart king doesn't tell his troops to keep on fighting when he sees he's about to lose the war. I decided to retreat like a king and take 2 weeks break from everything.

Before I do that I have to let the people who are around me aware know ,which is Aunty Becker at this moment. Firstly I told her to find a business idea which can bring money in the house and after I told her about my stress. She was interested in helping me out but I told her I want to do it by my own.

Tracy came by the house, she wanted to check up on me, I didn't want to chase her away, she was too caring about me. I decided to spend that week with Tracy and at the same time when I check my social media, I realize life goes on. It doesn't matter if you are sick or depressed at that time but life goes on. I wish things can't be easy for me but I have to understand pain is always there in the process of love and personality growth. I'm glad I knew this because it gives me hope that one day everything will be alright.

Monday morning,I decided I want to start to be productive , I had an enough break . I wanted to plan what I wanted to do with my money perhaps make a business plan . Before I do that I want to have a small talk , a method that I denial that I have been taught by my Uncle George . No one can cheat love and relationship , you can't fool someone who you gonna spend your whole life with . You can't fool someone one for a long period , it's impossible and eventually they will know .

I'm glad that I know I put my all in all my relationship, I know that the failure of my relationship it wasn't me but them . My problems is I wasn't meeting girls who are willing to commit , which is fine and my other problem is my two favorite people past on . I have to be strong and learn how to move on . Life contain pain and this goes along with relationship this is part of nature .

Why can't I find love ? Most people asked themselves this questions. I could say that we ask ourselves this because we don't appreciate what's infront of us . Once we don't get what we want/needs we tend to forget people who are really supporting us and trying every single thing for us .

Learn to appreciate if you really want to find love , appreciate yourself and people are with you . Small talks will be a tool for any personality growth . I hope everyone can understand my art of small talks .

Stay tuned for chapter 3 where Ben spends his whole pandemic lockdown with Tracy and discovered how his friend Max passed on.

Therefore chapter 2 will introduce the new character (female character) so on chapter 3 both character will have a chance to meet each other .

Description of the book

The book is about a young man who is walking a journey of mastering his own emotions and actions. He was always asking himself why can't he find love? He keeps on asking himself these questions and he wanted to understand what's wrong with him since he started to realizes that love is within him.

He had a bad experience dating girls who are not taking the relationship seriously and he decided to change his thoughts about always believing girls are the same. He applied methods that he created for himself for emotional control throughout his journey. One day his friend decided to host a party and he asked Ben to help him out with the preparation.

Ben discovered the girl of his dream at that house party. They shared a lot and did a lot during that whole weekend. Ben was so happy that he finally met someone who he can call his girlfriend. One day Ben saw his girlfriend in unexpected place with another guy(second boyfriend)

THE STORY CONTINUES when Ben starts to realize that emotions in long-term learning, he had to experience pain by losing people who are to close to him.

That's where he finally finds love.

Learn more about how Ben handled his scenario using the method he created for himself to master anything that has to do with emotions. This is a perfect book to help you master your own emotions, find love and grow your personality. The book also contains imagines of the characters during the scene.

About The Author

Lesiba Ignitiuas Kekana is also known by his stage name Kevin Kekana. He is born in South Africa(Limpopo in a small town called Mokopane). He is born on 25 October 1998. He is also using his pen name (Kevin Rabalao)as a brand to write small project books. In 2019 he wrote 4 books and he decided to take them down from the retailers because he felt like they are not good enough to be in his bookstore. He believes he is the most gifted author that ever walked on earth. His goal is to create the biggest online library with his 2 author brand names. He can write non-friction and friction books. He enjoys most, writing stories and educating others about his discoveries and research. His logo and signature is #IamKevinGotTheMainIdea

Vocabulary

Booze – Alcohol
Small talk – self talk/ self therapy
Popping- swallowing

Depression/suicidal helplines
Germany

+49 176 62371658[1]
Gotenstraße 74, 10829 Berlin, Germany[2]

1. https://www.google.co.za/search?q=germany+mental+health+services&client=safari&hl=en-za&sxsrf=ALiCzsbxql9UBb4y9hizPNw08PGGHDf8Mw%3A1653960985469&ei=GXGVYqWiHJiO8gLtqICQBQ&oq=germany+depression%2Fsuicide+helpline+for+german+citizens&gs_lcp=ChNtb2JpbGUtZ3dzLXdpei1zZXJwEAEYATIHCCMQsAMQJzIHCAAQRxCwAzIHCAAQRxCwAzIHCAAQRxCwAzIHCAAQRxCwAzIHCAAQRxCwAzIHCAAQRxCwAzIHCAAQRxCwA0oECEEYAFAAWABg-jVoAXAAeACAAQCIAQCSAQCYAQCgAQHAAQE&sclient=mobile-gws-wiz-serp

2. https://www.google.co.za/search?q=germany+mental+health+services&client=safari&hl=en-za&sxsrf=ALiCzsbxql9UBb4y9hizPNw08PGGHDf8Mw%3A1653960985469&ei=GXGVYqWiHJiO8gLtqICQBQ&oq=germany+depression%2Fsuicide+helpline+for+german+citizens&gs_lcp=ChNtb2JpbGUtZ3dzLXdpei1zZXJwEAEYATIHCCMQsAMQJzIHCAAQRxCwAzIHCAAQRxCwAzIHCAAQRxCwAzIHCAAQRxCwAzIHCAAQRxCwAzIHCAAQRxCwAzIHCAAQRxCwA0oECEEYAFAAWABg-jVoAXAAeACAAQCIAQCSAQCYAQCgAQHAAQE&sclient=mobile-gws-wiz-serp

United States of America

The **National Suicide Prevention Lifeline** is a United States-based suicide prevention[1] network of over 160 crisis centers that provides 24/7 service[2] via a toll-free hotline with the number **1 (800) 273-8255** (**TALK**). It is available to anyone in suicidal crisis or emotional distress

---

1. https://en.m.wikipedia.org/wiki/Suicide_prevention

2. https://en.m.wikipedia.org/wiki/24/7_service

Australian

Every 30 seconds, a person in Australia reaches out to Lifeline for help.

We are a national charity providing all Australians experiencing emotional distress with access to 24 hour crisis support and suicide prevention services.

Call 13 11 14

Canada

Https://www.crisisservicescanada.ca/call-us/

South Africa

Call :0800567567

Swiss

Https://www.143.ch/

Drug abusing counseling contact (Germany)

Altona

KODROBS Altona, Hohenesch 13-17, 22765 Hamburg, Phone: 040/3908640/ -41, Email: altona@kodrobs.de, Mon, Tue & Thu: 10 a.m. - 7 p.m., **ENG**

Kajal Frauenperspektiven, Substance abuse counselling for women, Haubachstraße 78, 22767 Hamburg, Phone: 040/ 3806987, Email: kajal@frauenperspektiven.de, Mon, Wed, Thu & Fri: 9 a.m. - 5 p.m., Tue: 2:30 p.m. - 5 p.m. Sat: 12 p.m. - 5 p.m., **ENG & FR**

Lukas Suchthilfezentrum, Luruper Hauptstr. 138, 22547 Hamburg, Phone: 040/ 970770, Mon & Thu: 9 a.m. - 6 p.m., Tue & Wed: 10 a.m. - 6 p.m., Fri: 10 a.m. - 3 p.m., **ENG**

Palette Bartelsstraße 12, 20357 Hamburg, Phone: 040/ 4302590, Email: bartesstrasse@palette-hamburg.de, Mon - Fri: 11 a.m. - 4 p.m., **ENG, FA**

Bergedorf

KODROBS Bergedorf, Lohbrügger Landstraße 6, 21031 Hamburg, Phone: 040/ 72160-38/ -39, Email: bergedorf@kodrobs.de, Mon, Tue & Fri: 10 a.m. - 5 p.m., Thu: 10 a.m. - 7 p.m.,**ENG, RU, ES**

Eimsbüttel

UKE University Hospital, Drug and alcohol walk-in clinic, Martinistraße 52, 20246 Hamburg, Phone: 040/ 741054217, Email: drogenambulanz@uke.de, open 24/7, **Interpreters for most languages can be arranged.**

Frauenperspektiven Substance abuse counselling for women, Charlottenstraße 26, 20257 Hamburg, Phone: 040/ 4329600, Email: beratungsstelle@frauenperspektiven.de, Mon, Wed & Thu: 10 a.m. - 4 p.m., Fri: 10 a.m. - 2 p.m., **ENG**

M.A.T. West, Elbgaustraße 83, 22523 Hamburg, Phone: 040/ 57193131, Email: mat-west@therapiehilfe.de, **ENG, FA**

Hamburg Mitte (Centre)

Büro für Suchtprävention, Repsoldstraße 4, 20097 Hamburg, Phone: 040/ 2849918-24, Email: hls@sucht-hamburg.de, **Interpreters for most languages can be arranged.**

Drob Inn St. Georg Directed specifically at opiate users, Besenbinderhof 71, 20097 Hamburg, Phone: 040/ 3999930, Email: drob.inn@jugendhilfe.de, Mon, Wed, Thu & Fri: 9 a.m. - 5 p.m., Tue: 2:30 p.m. - 5 p.m., Sat: 12 p.m. - 5 p.m.

KODROBS Wilhelmsburg, Weimarer Straße 83-85, 21107 Hamburg, Phone: 040/ 7216038/ -39, Email: wilhelmsburg@kodrobs.de, Mon, Tue & Thu: 10 a.m. - 7 p.m., Fri: 10 a.m. - 4 p.m., **ENG, RU, KU, TR**

Viva Billstedt - Take Care! Substance abuse counselling for young adults, Ruhmkoppel 14, 22119, Phone: 040/ 707020020 or 0151/ 59278822, Email: takecare-billstedt@jugendhilfe.de, open upon request, **ENG**

Hamburg Nord (North)

MobS Hamburg Nord Substance abuse counselling for young adults, Wischhöfen 1, 22415 Hamburg, Phone: 040/ 55440753, Email: mobs-nord@therapiehilfe.de, open upon request, **ENG, RU, POL, FA**

Harburg

OkayM.A.T. & Seehaus Harburg, Schlossmühlendamm 8-10, 21073 Hamburg, Phone: 040/ 7679490, Email: mat-harburg@therapiehilfe.de, Mon & Thu: 2 p.m. - 4 p.m., **ENG, FA**

STZ Harburg, Knoopstraße 37, 21073 Hamburg, Phone: 040/ 3347533-0, Email: lars.ehricke@martha-stiftung.de, Mon, Wed & Thu: 10 a.m. - 6 p.m., Tue: 2 p.m. - 6 p.m., Fri: 10 a.m. - 3 p.m., **ENG, ESP**

MobS Therapiehilfe, Cuxhavener Straße 386, 21149 Hamburg, Phone: 040/ 30384444, Email: mobs-harburg@therapiehilfe.de, open upon request, **ENG, POL, RU**

Wandsbek

Die Boje Suchthilfe, Brauhausstieg 15-17, 22041 Hamburg, Phone: 040/ 444091 or 040/ 7314949, Email: beratung@dieboje.de, Mon - Fri: 10 a.m. - 6 p.m., **ENG**

Die Brücke Eilbek, Conventstraße 14, 22089 Hamburg, Phone: 040/ 6683638, Tue: 3 p.m. - 5 p.m., **ENG**

Die Brücke Wandsbek, Walddörferstraße 337, 22047 Hamburg, Phone: 040/ 6683637, Email: info@ambulante-suchttherapie.de, Tue: 5 p.m. - 7 p.m., Thu: 3 p.m. - 5 p.m., **ENG, ESP**

Viva Wandsbek - Take Care! Substance abuse counselling for young adults, Bei den Höfen 23, 22043 Hamburg, Phone: 040/ 244242590 or 0177/ 2094549, Email: takecare@jugendhilfe.de, Mon - Wed: 10 a.m. - 6 p.m., Thu & Fri: 1 p.m. 6 p.m., **ENG**

Therapeutische Gemeinschaft Jenfeld (TGJ), Jenfelder Straße 100, 22045 Hamburg, Phone: 040/ 65409628, Email: info.aha@alida.de, Mon & Thu: 3 p.m. - 5 p.m., **ENG**

Australia

The phone service is available 24/ by calling (08) **9442 5000** or **1800 198 024** (toll-free for country callers).

Live Chat is also free of charge and available for Western Australian residents Monday to Friday 7.30am - 9pm, Saturday 9am - 7pm and

Sunday 11am - 6pm. Live Chat can be accessed here[1].

Email: alcoholdrugsupport@mhc.wa.gov.au

Web: alcoholdrugsupport.mhc.wa.gov.au[2]

---

1. https://www.mhc.wa.gov.au/about-us/our-services/alcohol-and-drug-support-service/live-chat-with-an-alcoholdrug-counsellor/

2. http://alcoholdrugsupport.mhc.wa.gov.au/

South African

Elim Clinic (Drug Abuse Treatment Centre)
  – **Call:** 011 975 2951 (Get Hours)
  – **Website:** www.elimclin.co.za[1]

---

1.   http://www.elimclin.co.za/

United States of America

DrugAbuse.com[1] hotline: Addiction Navigators on call 24/7 to help answer any questions related to drug abuse and support

- Al-Anon[2] and Ala-teen[3] hotline line: 800-356-9996 – Counselors provide support to teens and adults who are negatively impacted by alcohol addiction and provide resources to group therapy nearby for ongoing support.

- Substance Abuse and Mental Health Services Administration[4] (SAMHSA): 1-800-662-4357 – English/Spanish speaking counselors provide referrals to treatment facilities, support groups, and community-based services.

- National Suicide Prevention[5]: 1-800-273-8255 – Support to help those in crisis process their emotional distress and prevent suicide.

- Boys Town[6]: 1-800-448-3000 – Over 140 languages can be translated; they also provide a telecommunications device for the deaf (TDD) line for the speech and hearing impaired (1-800-448-1833).

- Drugfree.org[7]: call 855-378-4373 or text 55753 – Counselors provide support and education and guide you to the best course of action.

---

1. https://drugabuse.com/addiction/drug-abuse/hotlines/

2. https://al-anon.org/

3. https://al-anon.org/newcomers/teen-corner-alateen/

4. https://www.samhsa.gov/find-help/national-helpline

5. https://suicidepreventionlifeline.org/

6. https://www.boystown.org/hotline/Pages/default.aspx

7. https://drugfree.org/article/get-one-on-one-help/

Canada

Alberta[1] (Addiction Helpline, Alberta Health Services)

1-866-332-2322

British Columbia[2] (Alcohol and Drug Information and Referral Service)

1-800-663-1441

604-660-9382

Manitoba[3] (Addictions Foundation of Manitoba)

Adult services: 1-855-662-6605

Youth services: 1-877-710-3999

204-944-6200

New Brunswick[4] (Addiction Centres, Department of Health)

506-674-4300

Newfoundland and Labrador[5] (Addictions Services, Department of Health and Community Services)

1-888-737-4668

709-729-3658

Northwest Territories[6] (Department of Health and Social Services)

1-800-661-0844

867-873-7037

Nova Scotia[7] (Mental Health and Addictions Services, Nova Scotia Health Authority)

1-888-429-8167

Nunavut[8] (Kamatsiaqtut Help Line)

1-800-265-3333

867-979-3333

Ontario[9] (ConnexOntario)

1-866-531-2600

Prince Edward Island[10] (Addiction Services, Health PEI)

1-833-553-6983

902-368-4120

Quebec[11] (Drugs: help and referral)

1-800-265-2626

514-527-2626

Saskatchewan[12] (HealthLine, Ministry of Health)

811 or 1-877-800-0002

---

1. https://www.albertahealthservices.ca/amh/amh.aspx

2. http://www.bc211.ca/help-lines/#adirs

3. http://afm.mb.ca/programs-and-services/

4. http://www.gnb.ca/0378/centers-e.asp

5. https://www.health.gov.nl.ca/health/mentalhealth_committee/mentalhealth/treatment_centres.html

6. https://www.hss.gov.nt.ca/en/services/addictions/getting-help-addictions

7. http://www.nshealth.ca/mental-health-addictions

8. http://www.nunavuthelpline.ca/

9. http://www.connexontario.ca/

10. http://www.healthpei.ca/addictions

11. http://www.drogue-aidereference.qc.ca/

12. http://www.saskatchewan.ca/residents/health/accessing-health-care-services/healthline

306-766-6600
Yukon[13] (Mental Wellness and Substance Use Services, Health and Social Services)
1-866-456-3838 (for Yukon, Nunavut and NWT)
867-456-3838

---

13.   http://www.hss.gov.yk.ca/mwsu_communities.php

Swiss

+41 31 376 04 01
office@infodrog.ch

Source Reference

Https://youtu.be/QGQQ7pJQqHk[1]
https://youtu.be/hxCvJJv2vw8
https://www.hamburg.com/residents/social/11823820/addiction/
https://alcoholthinkagain.com.au/help/
https://www.samsosa.org/wp/help-lines/
https://americanaddictioncenters.org/rehab-guide/ alcohol-drug-hotline
https://www.ccsa.ca/addictions-treatment-helplines-canada
https://www.infodrog.ch/en/

HTTPS://EN.M.WIKIPEDIA.org/wiki/ National_Suicide_Prevention_Lifeline

HTTPS://WWW.LIFELINE.org.au

---

1. https://youtu.be/QGQQ7pJQqHk

Copyright

[Why can't I Find Love: Personality Growth] by [Lesiba Ignitiuas Kekana]
Published by [Garther Publishing]

Don't miss out!

Visit the website below and you can sign up to receive emails whenever Lesiba Ignitiuas kekana publishes a new book. There's no charge and no obligation.

https://books2read.com/r/B-A-ZNDU-HCKZB

BOOKS2READ

Connecting independent readers to independent writers.